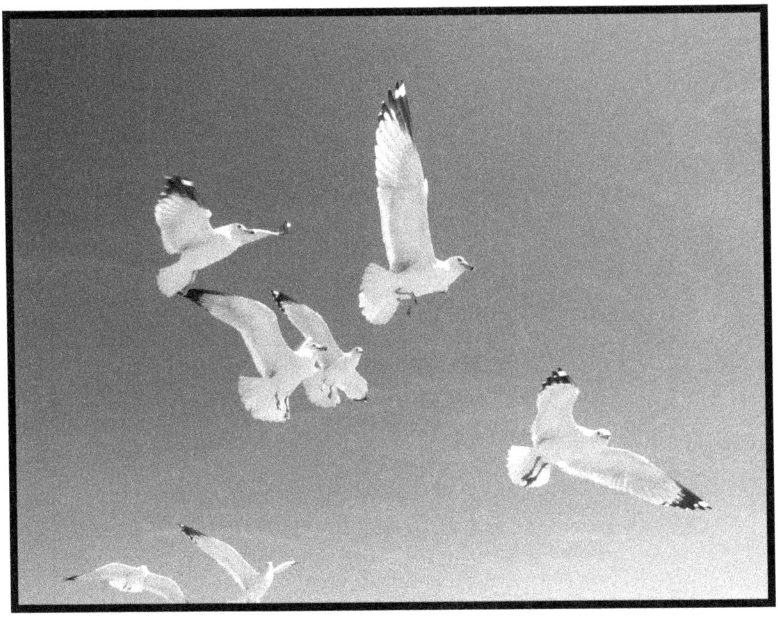

INSPIRED BY

MICHAEL C. WALKER

BALBOA
PRESS
A DIVISION OF HAY HOUSE

Copyright © 2018 Michael C. Walker.
Cover and Interior photos by Jennie Malone

All rights reserved. No part of this book may be used or reproduced by any means, graphic, electronic, or mechanical, including photocopying, recording, taping or by any information storage retrieval system without the written permission of the author except in the case of brief quotations embodied in critical articles and reviews.

Scriptures taken from the Holy Bible, New International Version®, NIV®. Copyright © 1973, 1978, 1984, 2011 by Biblica, Inc.™ Used by permission of Zondervan. All rights reserved worldwide. www.zondervan.com The "NIV" and "New International Version" are trademarks registered in the United States Patent and Trademark Office by Biblica, Inc.™

Author and Photographer Headshots by Tracey Mershon and James Jin

Balboa Press books may be ordered through booksellers or by contacting:

Balboa Press
A Division of Hay House
1663 Liberty Drive
Bloomington, IN 47403
www.balboapress.com
1 (877) 407-4847

Because of the dynamic nature of the Internet, any web addresses or links contained in this book may have changed since publication and may no longer be valid. The views expressed in this work are solely those of the author and do not necessarily reflect the views of the publisher, and the publisher hereby disclaims any responsibility for them.

The author of this book does not dispense medical advice or prescribe the use of any technique as a form of treatment for physical, emotional, or medical problems without the advice of a physician, either directly or indirectly. The intent of the author is only to offer information of a general nature to help you in your quest for emotional and spiritual well-being. In the event you use any of the information in this book for yourself, which is your constitutional right, the author and the publisher assume no responsibility for your actions.

Any people depicted in stock imagery provided by Getty Images are models, and such images are being used for illustrative purposes only.
Certain stock imagery © Getty Images.

Print information available on the last page.

ISBN: 978-1-9822-1067-0 (sc)
ISBN: 978-1-9822-1068-7 (e)

Balboa Press rev. date: 12/17/2018

Contents

Dedication vii
Preface ix
Chapter 1: Inspired by the Scripture of the Old Testament 1
Chapter 2: A Flock of Birds 15
Chapter 2A: Location, Location, Location 46
Chapter 3: Inspired by the Scripture of the New Testament 52
Epilogue 67
Acknowledgement 69

Dedication

To the person who sustained me in pre-life and through my stages of growth, Barbara Jean Harrison Walker. Momma, you are still watching over me.

And

To the extra two heartbeats, God gave me who sustain me now, Eleni Nicole and Melena Denise. My girls, I hope this work can be your legacy.

Preface

Everyone needs perspective. We are not the center of the universe. This is not the worst thing that can happen. The world is not going to come crashing down on our head and we do not have to carry the weight of the world on our shoulders.

These commonly used expressions are worth remembering as mantras. I carry many of them around with me in my head whenever I start feeling stress. The other thing I do is recall what I learned from my own psychotherapy; learning about my feelings in the past, that had taken me down a path of self-destructive behavior and poor decision-making. I also learned to pray. I do not mean a little. I prayed a lot. It is hard to trust an unseen God; but I believe God is with us; He supports us with grace, and always provides mercy whenever needed. As much as I pray over the smallest matters, I also pray a prayer of thanksgiving when God, in whom I give all my praise, helps to deal with my problems and to calm down when feeling stressed.

I am hopeful that you, the reader, will find solace along with your own method of achieving peace, enlightenment, and tranquility. Perhaps one of my short rhymes could become one of your mantras. I hope you see that our own strength is not enough to budge those things that weigh heavily upon us. We must rely on God's strength as well as his grace.

In my estimation the wisdom you can find in a book of inspiration is not meant to supplant the word of God with a shortcut to inspiration or to circumvent the Bible altogether. I think inspiration books offer another path on your journey to finding your way as you deal with life's daily challenges and obstacles.

Therefore, my objective with "Inspired by" is for you, the reader, to experience another way of relating Bible verses to your own life. I hope that you will recognize my source material right away and know that my words did not come from anywhere else but the Inspired Word of God. Maybe it will encourage you to read further and delve deeper into the Bible as well and my rhymes will inspire you in your daily walk with God. The following are passages I created from the New International Version of the Holy Bible.

The Author

CHAPTER 1

Inspired by the Scripture of the Old Testament

Inspired by the Scripture of the Old Testament

Even in the lowest depths of uncertainty, God's promise lifts us from the despair of any valley.

Inspired by Psalm 43:5

Despite what we may be facing; Jesus offers Himself, his heart is ever loving.

Inspired by Nehemiah 2:11-18

No matter how our lives may fare; the calming of Jesus is with us because he is always there.

Inspired by Psalms 32:1-11

In the most positive way you can employ, remember that each day is a gift with potential expectations and joy.

Inspired by Ecclesiastes 3:14

Blessings will happen to come in innumerable ways; God's goodness follows us all of our days.

Inspired by Psalm 107

Even with all that, we think we know, there is more knowledge to obtain, taking us where we need to go.

Inspired by Psalms 139:6-10

In order to discover what your life is all about, cherish all experiences and release all your doubt.

Inspired by Isaiah 41:10

In looking for where trust should be in the very first place, look for the one who provides all, asking for God's grace.

Inspired by Jeremiah 42:7-8

Each of us is creations made special; and more so by God's love for us, altogether remarkable.

Inspired by Genesis 1:26

When your act of kindness is random, it shows how your heart and head work in tandem.

Inspired by Ruth 2:10

The circumstances exist that we cannot understand; and our answered prayers are the miracles that happen by God's hand.

Inspired by Deuteronomy 10:21

While it may take a while for us to process, we are stronger daily through every distress.

Inspired by Job 23:10

In living our life determined not to buckle, we can balance stress with a timely chuckle.

Inspired by Psalms 126:2

Relying upon this force, it is God, a most powerful source.

Inspired by Job 26:14

In seeking prosperity, when the door may be closing, God provides a plan to keep us hoping.

Inspired by Jeremiah 29:11

While impatience conspires with anxiety in the stress it tries to create, patience is the virtue needed when we have to wait.

Inspired by Psalm 90:12

No matter where the winding path of life may go, God's presence helps us navigate it and grow.

Inspired by Joshua 1:9

For pure joy starts in the heart when praising, it leads to the encouragement to keep on singing.

Inspired by Psalm 95:1

In hope to live freely, draw closer to the cross, to help a spiritual journey.

Inspired by Judges 18:5-6

For the days that feel ugly, the solace of God assuages pain, inspiring feelings more bubbly.

Inspired by Job 16:5

What is truly clear and pure, God's love for us does endure.

Inspired by Isaiah 40:8

There is no greater gift and this you cannot pretend; it is the loyalty in being a true friend.

Inspired by Proverbs 20:6

Faced with diminished strength, what is a must? It is relying on God, in whom shall I trust.

Inspired by Daniel 6:26, Psalm 91:2

It is God's protection from dangers and harm, his covering us, keeping the body and the spirit warm.

Inspired by Zechariah 3:4

How we face our own obstacles is done best by demonstration; exemplifying the path for a future generation.

Inspired by Psalm 78:1-8

Concerning those defining chapters in a life story, rejoicing is praise to God for the glory.

Inspired by Psalm 8:1-8

Even when it appears that we have so far to go, the journey moves forward as the progress will show.

Inspired by Numbers 33:2

It is a gift held in each sunrise and sunset view, a picturesque scene in living color and beauty, too.

Inspired by Psalm 148:3

With so much to weigh and discern, good guidance is helpful with so much in life to learn.

Inspired by Isaiah 43:18-19

Avoid the strife that may linger; end the pettiness that often leads to anger.

Inspired by Proverbs 20:3

There is no reason to feel alone in any space, as God is present in every place.

Inspired by Genesis 28:16

There may not be a perfect cure for what is broken inside; but the expression of empathy may help stem the tide.

Inspired by Psalm 51

Before any endeavor should proceed, request God's blessing and for what that project may ultimately need.

Inspired by Jeremiah 29:11-13

In search of the anchor on which to lock, look to the foundation because God is that rock.

Inspired by Psalm 18:2

A joyous spirit is a wondrously miraculous thing; a reason to praise God and sing.

Inspired by 2 Chronicles 20:21

Through the frenzy, the hustle of crowds, serenity exists found in the wonder among the clouds.

Inspired by Job 37: 13-15

When what is offered to both aid and comfort, it follows the example of the Good Shepherd.

Inspired by Isaiah 40:11

It is the wisdom with the greatest influence; when it offers solace, it is continuous.

Inspired by Deuteronomy 31:8-9

The blessings are that spiritual food; showing God's hand is very good.

Inspired by Genesis 1:24-31

From God, spiritual food will nourish; strengthening the body and soul in order to flourish.

Inspired by Ezekiel 34:14

Where the core of misunderstandings resides; patience and empathy destroys what divides.

Inspired by Joshua 7:1-12

God's does not parse love among His creations, casting them aside; that abundance to them, He will not deny.

Inspired by Genesis 45:1-11

No matter the heavy burden, what can be best; keeping things in perspective and insure the body has rest.

Inspired by Exodus 23:10-13

In prayer, ask for forgiveness for yourself and for others, seeing them as friends, sisters and brothers.

Inspired by Exodus 32:32

Confronting injustice is a relentless fight; even when standing alone for what is truly right.

Inspired by Genesis 4:1-12

When God blesses with His grace, it is His way of speaking face to face.

Inspired by Exodus 33:7-14

While in the midst of trials and burdens of everyday life, God remains steadfast to aid in handling the strife.

Inspired by Psalm 66:10

While the Lord's sovereignty is forever near, we walk on heights with nothing to fear.

Inspired by Habakkuk 3:19

In God's refuge, our spirit happily sings; covered like the feathers under a bird's wings.

Inspired by Psalm 91:4

Just as there is a reason for every word to rhyme, everything comes to season only in its own time.

Inspired by Ecclesiastes 3:1

CHAPTER 2

A Flock of Birds

Eastern Bluebird Sketch by the late BJ Walker, 1933-2015

A Flock of Birds

There is something fascinating about birds. They seem to be the most free of God's creations because they can escape the law gravity that keep us humans earthbound.

To escape in order to be free occupies our minds whether we are in the drudgery of a task or even worse, held captive or enslaved.

The inspired word of God shows us unequivocally that He valued the creation of birds. The Old Testament mentions specifically that the creation of birds was very prominent.

My late mother found comfort in watching them as they meticulously went about their chores of nesting and gathering food for their young.

In her later years, she tried to capture one of her favorites, the Eastern Bluebird in her sketchbook. It was unfinished in her mind, but to me, I think she caught enough of its essence.

It is my distinct honor to include this and one other sketch of hers in my book. I drew inspiration from my mother's art in developing the poems that are an homage to gentleness and cheerfulness of birds.

Genesis 1:21 says, "So God created the great creatures of the sea and every living thing with which the water teems and that moves about in it, according to their kinds, and every winged bird according to its kind. And God saw that it was good (NIV)."

My collaborator captured dozens of portrait, landscape and macro shots of these beautiful flying creatures and for the next few pages, it is my pleasure to present Jennie Malone's outstanding photography and my poems.

I hope that in the next two sections you will draw as much inspiration as God found what was good in the creation of birds. Moreover, I hope your spirit will enjoy a flight of escape from whatever may be dragging you down; and thus you will be as free as a bird.

A Flock of Birds

Sing Your Song

Mister Yellowbird don't go away too soon
Not before, you sing your brand new tune.
That song that lifts me up as if I am a diamond in the sky,
Melody makes me feel like I can soar and fly.
Mister Yellowbird you bring so much joy to me,
Please sing that song I want to feel free.

Sint Michiel, Curacao

Take Flight and Soar

Little parakeet as I see you take flight and soar,
How I wish I could follow you even more.
From limb to limb, tree by tree,
You make your way so effortlessly.
Little parakeet please stay put for just a little while,
As I admire you longer, you make me smile.

Brooklyn, NY

A Tit for Tat

My little tit with a caterpillar on your mind,
That morsel of food you hope you may find.
Snatching seeds is the one thing you must do
When worms are eluding you.
My little tit you flutter around in such a manic and furious way.
I would like to photograph you, I beseech thee, please stay.

Tokyo, Japan

Relax Yourself

The little birdy chased my blues away,
Singing merry songs along the way.
The weight of the world on my weary head,
my little birdy chirped and chirped and this is what he said,
"Where has your smile gone from your face?
Make yourself another one to take its place.
Stop carrying your troubles around in your head.
"You relax yourself," the little birdy said.
I am glad I had a friend like him,
who pulled me up and made me feel less grim.

Soto, Curacao

Drop in and Make My Day

Good morning my diminutive friend,
Thank you for coming by and dropping in.
I know you have a busy day ahead,
You have worms to catch,
I have stuff, too, and that said,
I will get myself up anyway,
Thanks again for serenading me,
You have made my day.

Newport, KY

The Morning Wake Up Call

When I slowly awaken to hear your familiar call,
I should rise from my slumber, ready to stand tall.

Your song comes in sharper and now I am awake,
My pillow can't even damper it for goodness sake.

It is not that I am cross with you in any way;
it is time I got up and started on my day.

So enjoy the snack of seed and millet I left for you in the feeder.
It ought to carry you until you reach your
nest in that beautiful cedar.

I cannot wait to hear from you, so come back soon.
I am looking forward to that beautiful morning tune.

Noord, Aruba

These Seeds for You from Me

My itty friend, whenever you come by
looking for your daily bread,
I hope you would land at my special place where you are fed.

I hope you find in the seeds that are there,
as my generosity shows, I really care.

After you take off, I hope you visit I really do,
I will have more seeds, perhaps even a worm for you.

St. Petersburg, Russia

Sharing Our Sky

In all of this total ecology,
Birds occupy significance,
In addition, that is plain to see since they live in every tree.

Without the birds what would occupy the sky?
The clouds would be lonely; I know they would cry.

Birds have been with us forever and a day,
We could not exist without them in any way.

Let us not them for granted we should appreciate them.
When they want into our lives, let us invite them in.

Leave some crumbs for them, maybe a seed or two,
Just a few they can quickly chew.

If you have the time to build a little shelter,
It will keep out of harm from the stormy weather.

Be tolerant and by opening your heart, you receive this grace,
God made all his creatures to live freely in this earthly space.

Delray Beach, FL

You Don't Say

I stare at you and you twitch and turn,
do you even see me as I try to discern?
I know what you look like in my human view.
Am I as vividly colorful and brilliant to you?

Your language is a melodic series of twerps here and tweets there.
I wish I could follow you as you glide in the air.

If I could interpret the sound you and your cousins make in trees,
Our talks would endure with the greatest of ease.

I will keep a watchful eye on you my fine little friend,
in the hope my understanding of you will never end.

Soto, Curacao

One Who is Greater Than You and Me

Here is my thought and I hope you understand,
How I can, I hold you in the palm of my hand.

There is one greater than me that can hold me, too.
He created me and he created you.

It was his desire that we both would thrive,
In this place where we to need to survive.

While I have dominion over you and that is plain to see.
The maker of all of this has greater
authority that towers over me.

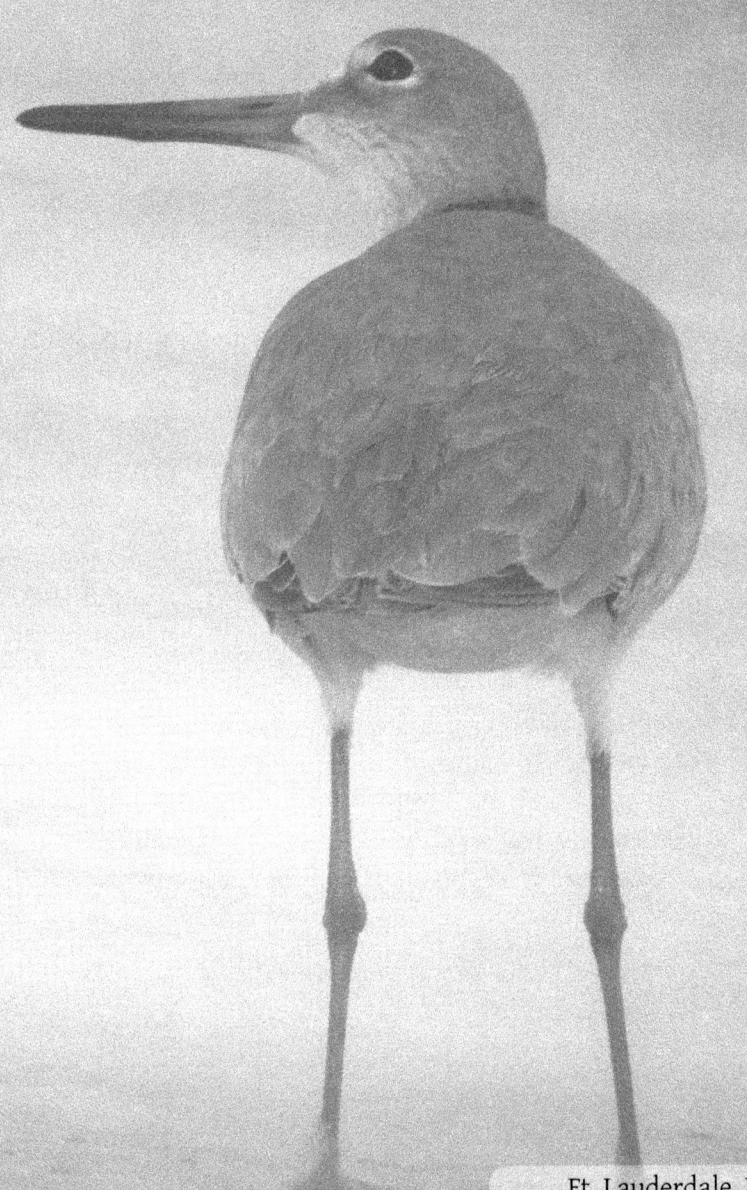

Ft. Lauderdale, FL

Inspired By | 37

Staying Grounded

When you have a way out and all you have to do is flee,
Not having such means really bothers me.

My feathered friends can escape that snare,
Wings flapping, then soaring;
Free to go just about anywhere.

When I ponder deeply how far I might fly,
I think of Icarus, who fell from the sky.

It's just fantasy and upon further review,
If God created me that way, I would have those wings, too.

If I had my druthers, I would want to stick around,
Keeping my feet planted firmly on the ground.

Ft. Lauderdale, FL

Inspired By | 39

Is the Grass Greener?

Are you aware how generous your Maker
has been to you and your kind.
Endowing you with gifts, hardly any other
species on their own could find.

As you rise into the air, it occurs to me,
How very liberating you have it being so free.

We who go about our way on legs upright,
Dreaming we could join you and fly out of sight.

I guess the grass is always greener when I fantasize about you.
I wonder if you ever wonder what it is like to be human, too.

Sarasota, FL

Looking for Your Tiny Prey

Tap, tap, tap, goes my friend,
Off on another worm hunt once again.

The search is long, so it is time for a rest,
He has found a birch tree with a twiggy nest.

I do not know long he plans to stay.
I hope he finds that elusive prey.

Tap, tap, tap, he's flown the coop;
Joining the formation of his airborne group.

Alexandria Bay, NY

Your Perfect Song

There is nothing to make me more proud,
Than hearing from my feathered friend, singing loud.

I know when they nest; it is not for long,
I just enjoying listening to their melodic song.

Those leafy trees make for a perfect situation,
For a brief rest a while, as I capture this composition.

I do not know if they even realize
What a treat they are for my very own eyes.

Noord, Aruba

CHAPTER 2A

Location, Location, Location

{- Tree Sketch by the late BJ Walker, 1933-2015}

Montego Bay, Jamaica

Nassau, The Bahamas

48 | *Michael C. Walker*

Helsinki, Finland

Newport, KY

Jamestown, KY

Delray Beach, FL

Delray Beach, FL

CHAPTER 3

Inspired by the Scripture of the New Testament

Inspired by the Scripture of the New Testament

Situations may not be as hopeless as they might seem, given how faith proves powerful in the most extreme.

Inspired by Ephesians 1:15-23

God's wisdom is always near; following it comes down to what we choose to hear.

Inspired by 1 Corinthians 2: 6-16

For the abandoned, of whom we may not be aware, the gift of God's love is there; it is just waiting for us to share.

Inspired by 1 John 4:7-8

As a life increases in worth and in value, consider that when living in Christ, that creation brand new.

Inspired by 2 Corinthians 5:17

The collective chances of success are assuredly better; especially when positive energy to works in concert together.

Inspired by Romans 8:28

Precious under God's eternal light, there is nothing hidden from His almighty sight.

Inspired by Hebrews 4:12-13

With God's powerful love always reassuring, it is no doubt that it is just as enduring.

Inspired by 2 Corinthians 20:6

As deep shadows in our lives may reach, the shadows pass with charitable and thoughtful speech.

Inspired by Matthew 15:11

Being a blessing to others is a pleasure; sharing not only time, but your talents, your true treasure.

Inspired by 2 Corinthians 4:1-7

For the ones whose generosity on which we may often lean, they are personal angels and many times, they are unseen.

Inspired by 1 Peter 1:12

For who we are and for what we do; Jesus loves us, his children, to the highest value.

Inspired by Romans 8:35, 39

Sins and transgressions may hang from our neck like an albatross, but Jesus bore them all, nailed to the cross.

Inspired by I Peter 2:24

Feeling lowly, nearly invisible thinking no one can see us; Compassion arrives emulating the love of Jesus.

Inspired by Colossians 3:12

Peace conquers the hate that wants to destroy; those bleak things replaced by joy.

Inspired by Philippians 4:8

In our sins God may not condone, we are redeemed by the death of Jesus, meant to atone.

Inspired by I John 1:8-2:2

For the slate we would like to wipe clean, Jesus is the strength on that we can lean.

Inspired by John 13:25

Jesus prepares a compassionate place, comforting us from the anxieties we face.

Inspired by John 14:3

With love in our lives, God enhances, it is why we should give thanks in all circumstances.

Inspired by 1 Thessalonians 3:18

Though we are flawed, we remain special in God's eyes; saved by His grace, we are not lowly, so rise.

Inspired by 1 Corinthians 15:55

In the faith we possess, we gain a connection to God with unlimited access.

Inspired by Ephesians 3:7-13

We are precious in God's sight; give praise to His Glory, it is a brilliant light.

Inspired by John 9

Every day when we step out on faith, mysteries unfold, allowing us to live life just being bold.

Inspired by I Thessalonians 1:8

Facing our day, we are intrepid, even circumspect; but guiding us is God's grace because it is perfect.

Inspired by I Timothy 1:13-14

During our daily race, we simply should not lose, if participating in it is what we choose.

Inspired by Hebrews 12:1

Love expressed is a fragrant bouquet; permeating sweetly in every way.

Inspired by John 13:34-35

No matter what happens in our daily living, others will benefit if we are unselfish in our sharing.

Inspired by 2 Corinthians 9:7

If the voice is continuously speaking, consider how much more the contribution with only listening.

Inspired by James 1:19

Even with those things given seemingly so small, they prove to be beneficial after all.

Inspired by James 1:17

When giving up feels like the only avenue, it prevents the effort of seeing things through.

Inspired by Galatians 6:9

For those in need of a helping hand, could use gentle empathy of someone who will understand.

Inspired by 1 Peter 3:8

This is a sign that God's love remains with us; coming in the sacrifice and resurrection of Jesus.

Inspired by John 3:16

Compassion and kindness can mean so much, the miracle felt in a simple and gentle touch.

Inspired by Matthew 8:1-4

It is the way to aspire to live; regarding transgressions, learn to forgive.

Inspired by Colossians 3:13

Demonstrate love and care, precious gifts and ones that people ought to share.

Inspired by 1 Peter 5:7

The belief in the very one who advocates best is always for us, He comes in the form of Christ Jesus.

Inspired by 1 John 2:1-2

Acting as Christ is not in endless talk; but more precisely in a purposeful walk.

Inspired by 1 John 2:6

It is the transformation worth waiting to see; it is growth and living the life meant to be.

Inspired by 2 Corinthians 3:18

Sharing gifts and offering help is the better strategy, eliminating selfishness and jealousy.

Inspired by Philippians 2:3

True heroism is honorable not in showy way; but with deep humility sacrificing every day.

Inspired by Matthew 6:1-6

In order to personally cope and manage, face the obstacles that often challenge.

Inspired 1 Peter 4:12-13

Just as spirits starts falling, that is when God is calling.

Inspired by John 10:3

As the search for tranquility may be a sought after need, the path to Jesus is where that search will lead.

Inspired by Acts 8:36-39

Nothing created by God is useless, as it rose into immortal life when it becomes breathless.

Inspired by 1 Corinthians 15:42-44

What should be with one another and hoping it will not cease mutual respect and a bond of peace.

Inspired by Ephesians 4:1-6

Saved by grace in order to thrive; discover the purpose in being alive.

Inspired by Ephesians 2:1-10

For a positive attitude to last for a while, always look for any reason to smile.

Inspired by 1 Thessalonians 5:9-11

Like music blending in concert to produce a symphony, it blends best when unified with harmony.

Inspired by Romans 12:3-8

To those of high regard serving the lowly, imitate the actions of the one most Holy.

Inspired by John 13:3-17

There is no better way for caring, than being authentic especially praying.

Inspired by James 5:16

Though a work in progress is unfinished, in the eyes of God, there is no blemish.

Inspired by Romans 7:14-25

In an effort not to be a distraction, the best display of faith is to use a little discretion.

Inspired by James 2:18

To make changes do not stew or complain; be rid of things, it is the momentum needed to maintain.

Inspired by 1 Peter 1:22-2:5

Everywhere in God's kingdom, thankfully, all of us can celebrate freedom.

Inspired by Romans 6:15-23

Before bold trepidation allows one to do their worst, send forth prayers allowing God to go ahead first.

Inspired by 1 John 4:7-21

Consider in practical ways as Jesus would, which is considering what is ultimately good.

Inspired by Philippians 3:1-11

Epilogue

The one word that speaks loudest to me about God's love is mercy.

I recall when I was very young how easily my brothers and I used to roughhouse. Since my oldest brother is eight years older than I am and my youngest, two years younger than me, he would take us both on two on one.

I do not know how he managed it, but he was quickly able to pin the both of us. My Achilles heel was the fact I was extremely ticklish and he knew exactly where to weaken me and I would go from gleefully laughing to begging with tears streaming down my face for mercy.

He would relent after a while and show me a bit of mercy. I am wistful about this because it was a long ago memory and no matter how misty and mossy the memory becomes over time, it still makes me smile.

I sometimes wonder what happens to that supply of mercy we have in our own possession. Do we have a ready stream of it that will flow like a river or is it like the last few drops that fall intermittently from a water faucet not completely turned off?

Certainly if one has an advantage of both size and strength over someone, they have the power to exert themselves without regard of mercy or they could easily relent and release the powerless and weak from their captivity.

Consider the mercy Almighty God shows us each day with His presence, his compassion and his love. He relents and releases us from captivity of our torment in many ways.

When our original covenant was broken with God, He saved his greatest act of mercy towards us by giving us Jesus, His only Begotten Son, as written in John 3:16.

My hope for you is that if you are feeling pinned down by something that has you begging for mercy, it will flow like a river and be a bounty for you. In equal measure, I pray that if you have the choice, your mercy flows upon someone who needs it from you the most.

Acknowledgement

I acknowledge the following people whose inspiration has guided me in my faith walk. Their influence and presence has proven to be most significant in my life. It guided me in my writing of this book and their friendship is very essential to me:

Dr. Aaron Gabriel Shames	April Boddie	Catherine Harmeyer
Shellie Smith	Edward T. Harrison, Jr.	Emily Mislan
Gia T. Cacalano	Bonnie Faber	Adam Kelkis
Fred Johnson	The Late Sister Diane Guy	Lauren Stanley
Annie Gilstrap	Serenity Fisher	Soroya Hill
Rosalie Brillantes Rodriguez	Bobby Fisher	Keith Harrison Walker
Kimberlea A. Jones	Lindsay Boyce	Christina Walker
Michelle Gabriele	Jane Gardner	Dr. Christine Hebert
Christopher O. James	Steven Cyrs	Dr. Robert Martinez and Family

Salvatore Scafidi	Sara Williams	Kiesha Morrison-Poole
Joy Martin	Ethel Holmes	Noreen Baker
Robert Nerius	Theresa Magyar	David M. Smith
Father Daniel Beeman	The Late Father Thomas J. Quinlan	Larry Duncan
Father Matthias Lusembo	Monsignor Walter Carlin Barrett	Patricia Wilgus
Father James Curran	Jim Parke	Brian Malone
Father Cristiano Brito	Stephen J. Hammond	J.W. Rickert

and Marcus C. Walker, Sr.